The Ogre's Wife

THE OGRE'S WIFE

poems

Ron Koertge

 RED HEN PRESS | *Pasadena, CA*

Book design and layout by Christina Kharbertyan

Library of Congress Cataloging-in-Publication Data
Koertge, Ronald.
  [Poems. Selections]
  The ogre's wife : poems / Ron Koertge—First edition.
    pages ; cm.
  ISBN 978-1-59709-723-9
  I. Title.
  PS3561.O347O35 2013
  811'.54—dc23
                    2013004265

The Los Angeles County Arts Commission, the National Endowment for the Arts, the City of Pasadena Cultural Affairs Division, Sony Pictures Entertainment, the Los Angeles Department of Cultural Affairs, and the Dwight Stuart Youth Fund partially support Red Hen Press.

First Edition
Published by Red Hen Press
www.redhen.org

Acknowledgments

Grateful acknowledgments are made to the editors of the following journals in which these poems first appeared: 5 *AM*, "Icarus," "Parking Lot at 7th and Main"; *Bryant Literary Review*, "Alone," "Open at 10:00 A.M."; *Court Green*, "Medication Guide"; *The Horn Book Magazine*, "Little, Small, Wee Bear," "The Ogre's Wife"; *Jacket*, "Three Haibun"; *Malpais Review*, "Museum of Science & Industry"; *Oh No*, "Rumplestiltskin"; *Poems & Plays*, "Trojan Pony," "Walt Whitman in North Hollywood"; *Rattling Wall*, "Photo"; and *Slipstream*, "Cincinnati, 1947."

Thanks to the keen-eyed
Bianca Richards
Jan Uebersetzig
Chris Heppermann

Table of Contents

III

I

Little Red Riding Hood:
A Memoir

I'm not little anymore: childbirth, motherhood, butter
and honey, salsa and chips. Sour cream.

But I was a knockout then. None of the girls in the village
liked me. "If you ever run into a wolf that talks," they said
from under their drab caps, "it means you'll be lucky in love."

I knew they were lying, but the idea seized me:
a talking beast. So I set out in my riding costume.
I was a flame playing across the forest floor.

O, the eagerness of him, the gusts of his breath. To take
off my hood and dress, my anklets and shoes, the gauzy
underwear pressed upon me by the milliner's son.

To slide into my grandmother's sachet-laden bed
with him and play what-strong-arms-what-strong-legs-
what-white-teeth.

Now I'm a matron or at least matronly. I have children—
one a gymnast, one a soccer player. I drive a Toyota.

My husband still finds me desirable. I like it when
he slobbers. It reminds me of my trip down the wolf's
gullet. Sometimes

I think about the woodsman. Without him I'd be dead.
But when I remember the wolf, snipped open like a pouch,
I cry and my husband stops what he is doing and kisses
my eyes, the better to see him with.

TRAFFIC

I was kissing this woman
I didn't know very well.

"I really like this," she said.
"My husband never kisses
me. He does you know
what and that's that."

"I like this, too," I told her.
"The other is just okay."

From the cars on her
street, one after another,

love songs. Some brutal
and full of bad grammar,

others enamored of
themselves.

FIELD TRIP

They're good kids, rich and sheltered. Dutifully
they hold the hand of the boy or girl beside them.

They file out of the library with their teacher,
and there's Death eating a sandwich.

They can't help but stare. He's sitting right where
that raccoon was a couple of months ago.

Their teacher told them all about raccoons, a medium-
sized mammal whose original habitats were
deciduous forests.

"Who is that person?" asks Tyler who will never grow
up to be a senator and, in fact, will never grow up at all.

"Look at this!" the teacher cries pointing to an anthill
at her feet. The children stare politely at the raised mound

and the lines of workers, some carrying crumbs twice
their size, others the bodies of their fallen comrades.

Parking Lot at 7ᵗʰ and Main

Sometimes when I see a room for rent—
and it's always just a room, never an apartment—
I think about living there.

I wouldn't have a dog or a cat, a fish
or a cactus. I guess I'd sleep on the floor.

It's a horrible thought, really. No wife
or friends. Not a chair or a book. I don't know
what I think I'd do.

Wait, maybe, for a light to go on or off,
for a panel in the wall to open and reveal
the staircase to an unimagined world.

Roadside Crèche

Traditionally, Gaspar, Melchior and Balthasar
show up with their exotic gifts, though the Bible
does not name them and some scholars believe

the Chinese sage Liu Shang might have attended
with a gift of silk rather than myrrh. Or even
better—fireworks. This Christ child's missing

fingers suggest he already has some experience
with cherry bombs or Red Devil Ground Blasters.
In this crèche, though, the magi have yet to arrive.

There are no camels, just a plaster zebra peering
over Mary's shoulder, and Joseph must have stepped
out for milk or cigarettes. The weight of adoration

has fallen onto the shoulders of a single, scowling
shepherd with binoculars slung around his neck.
Is he still keeping watch over his flock despite

the mischievous star that lured him from his
tranquil hillside and utterly bewildered dog?

CINCINNATI, 1947

Jackie Robinson knew what he was in for when he signed
with the Dodgers. He'd talked to a few other Negroes.
They said it was the same everywhere so he might as well
get paid to take it.

Teammates passed around petitions to get rid of him.
He sat by himself. Ate alone. Sometimes on the road
he'd go into Darktown just to shoot some pool and be
slightly famous.

One day in Cincinnati, the fans spit on him, swear
at him, throw bottles. Pee Wee Reese trots over, puts
his arm around Robinson's shoulders and the stands
go quiet.

Reese says, "Don't let 'em get to you."
Robinson replies, "What the fuck do you know?"

Reese's hand comes off the shoulder and the jeers start
again. He puts it back and they stop. Off/on. Off/on.

Robinson could tell Reese liked it. The power he had
even if at that moment he was barely batting .200
and every cheap twist in every city said he wasn't
called Pee Wee for nothing.

Trivial

The word comes from tri + via: three
roads. And it came to mean things of no
importance because that's where women
would stop and talk.

A man made that up, don't you think? He'd
be riding a fine horse, his head full of important
thoughts about his life, his sons, his money.

There would be these women standing where
three roads met filling the air with weather
and babies and recipes.

He would look them up and down, and lick his
fat lips as they whispered to each other how easy
it would be to make it look like somebody else
killed him, some man driven by the things men
talk about—envy, rage, revenge.

Rumplestiltskin

Music from indoors, a punch line
about nuns, smokers in the cave
of the garage point their doobie
at the moon.

A shirtless boy canters by, his
girlfriend on his back. The cranky
niece leaves a trail of Saltines as

she disappears into the part
of the yard held in place by two
dignified trees. Here comes
someone

who wants us inside for an
incoherent prayer and potatoes
white as talcum.

We're agreeable but in no hurry.
The nachos make their rounds.
Somebody opens a beer with
his teeth.

There's a bougainvillea next
door that's red enough to be
annoying. "All right. We're
coming in,"

someone lies. But really we're not.
It's lovely here. The straw of the day,
bushel after bushel of it, slowly
turns to gold.

PATRIMONY

Someone at our church got rich
quick, covered his wife with mink
and bought a country house.

Driving home my father said,
"A goddamned country house."
He pounded the dashboard.

"Ronnie, do me a favor. When
you grow up, show that s.o.b.
Who does he think he is!"

Recently I was in a country house.
I read by the fireplace and people
listened. I ate at the long table

and thanked the hostess. Over
her shoulder I saw my father's
angry face on the other side

of the beveled glass. He beat
on the French doors with both
fists as a small dog trotted that

way and began to bark furiously
until someone in an apron scooped
him up and carried him away.

Occasional Poems

Recently I wrote "I Buy Myself a Shirt" and "On Getting
Out of Bed." That's why it's so great to be a poet today:
Everything is fair game. Basically I'm self-employed
with nobody to please but myself.

In the past, there was a court poet. He got out of bed, too,
and probably put on a shirt, but he couldn't write about that.
His subjects were momentous: marriage, birth, death.

Take a royal wedding, for example. There sat the king
horny and bored, stuffed with peacock and swan. The poem
had to be perfect—part epithalamion, part bawdy limerick.

And nine months later, a poem on birth. For an heir,
an eclogue in Virgilian hexameters with references to
a golden age. For a girl, well—something pretty.
A song of praise but tempered with regret.

When it came to death, a lingering illness helped. Time
to strike just the right note. Black-clad parishioners
should nod and weep silently. The meter deliberate,
to match the tolling of bells.

Sudden death was the worst. News brought by horseback.
The messenger pacing in the courtyard, children shrieking
and taunting each other while upstairs the poet mutters
and chews his quill.

"Never Let Your Reader's Attention Wander."

Writer's Digest

In *Cat People*, Oliver marries Irena, but she says they can't
go on a honeymoon because of a gypsy curse. If they have
sex, she'll turn into a panther and kill him. In one of the great
understatements in film he says, "I wish you'd told me this
before we were married." That's not true. He's a modern
husband, so he sends her to a shrink. Oliver has a co-worker,
Alice, with tremendously hot pants. Actually, no. She's just
a normal gal who likes Oliver. When he tells Alice about
Irena and the curse she says, "Holy shit!" Not really. Alice
would never talk like that. In 1942 nobody in the movies
talked like that. Meanwhile, the shrink can't seem to think
of anything but Irena and the way she padded into his office
and curled up by the fire. Ooops. Not the part about the fire.
At their next session, he tries to kiss her and she claws him
to death. Now she has to die. The Legion of Decency says
so: virtue rewarded, evil punished. The Catholics even
banned "excessive and lustful kissing." Well, that's why
I frequent prostitutes. An hour of excessive kissing for $75.
$65 with the discount regulars get. Just kidding. I don't
go to massage parlors or houses set back off the road with
covered parking. I'm just trying, dear reader, to keep you
interested. This is poetry, not an exciting movie with huge
Cokes to keep everybody alert. But you're still with me,
aren't you? I'm so glad. Just a few more sentences. At
the end of the movie, Irena dies at the zoo by panthercide.
Alice and Oliver find her body and he says, "She never
lied to us." Well, she didn't have readers with a dozen
other things on their minds. And he only had Alice
who, with Irena out of the way, unbuttons her blouse
to reveal a florid tattoo set off by a midnight black
bra. Not really. I just made that up.

AUBADE

At eight a.m. what could be better
than Bette Davis starring in *The Letter*,

with Herbert Marshall and his ever-puckered lips
as her loyal husband, Mr. Pussy-Whipped.

Here's the story in a nutshell: it's
Malaya, it's hot, Bette Davis has this itch

only sexy Geoff can scratch. But he marries
"that native woman!" What a catastrophe

for Bette, so she shoots him a few times
and when the cops come she offers gin & lime

and says Geoff tried to force himself on her.
What else could she do? Her honor

was at stake. Of course. The trial should be a breeze.
Until an unctuous clerk and part-time leech

produces her incriminating letter
proving Geoff was not a drunken lecher.

Money changes hands, Bette is acquitted.
Then Herbert Marshall learns his wife's a bitch.

He cries like the douche bag he is and forgives
Bette who's fed up and ready for the shiv.

Gladly she steps into the moon-shady
garden where she's stabbed by the Dragon Lady.

The credits roll. The End. I stand and stretch.
Outside, the day is black-and-white, a sketch

of the afternoon to come. There are bills
to pay, errands that have to be run (pills

from Rite-Aid, shirts from Clean & Brite)
and someone in a truck to fix my satellite.

There must be twenty things I need to get done,
but look what's on next! It's *Mr. Skeffington*.

Hat

When the final is over, Carlos hands me
something and says, "Merry Christmas.
This'll keep your big old bald head warm."

It's no snowflake ski cap, that's for sure.
This one is the color of quicksand.

Carlos and his friends wear theirs
as they stand in the hall, all their hearts
on one sleeve and that rolled up to reveal
a brutal tattoo.

Now when I go to bed I put on what my wife
calls the Carlos hat. It does keep my big old
bald head warm

and in my dreams I don't take shit
from nobody.

ANOTHER MUSE IN STAINED PAJAMAS

William Carlos Williams wrote about what he saw and did.
As a physician, childbirth entered his work and accidents
involving a tractor or combine.

Let's watch him today making rounds at the contagious hospital.
He's bald and wears glasses, his face partly hidden by one
of those surgical masks.

He makes a point of touching patients and chatting with them
before having coffee alongside a pretty nurse in a white room
with white furniture scrupulously wiped down twice a day.

"Goodbye, everybody," he says, then walks to his car which
is not that big or new, but the motor turns over easily. He lets
it idle against the cold. He can't stop thinking about that hopeless
case whose bed was against the wall by the window. WCW
reaches for a piece of paper.

Immediately the dying man opens the door on the passenger's side
and gets in. Look how that noxious breath clouds the windshield.

Sanguine

It's about your tests. There might be a problem.
Or not. It's hard to tell sometimes.
The lab technicians are often on break.
There are stories about mix-ups concerning blood
and X-rays that look like maps drawn by children.
But just stories. We really don't know.

So come in. Just so you will know
for sure if there is/isn't a problem.
Feel free to bring your precious children
if you have any. Patients do this sometimes.
The young can be sanguine about the sight of blood
unless it terrifies them and they completely break

down. Even that's okay with us. It's a break
from pretending that we really know
anything. Sometimes we can't tell jam from blood.
And, let's face it, that can be quite a problem
though jam will come out of rayon. Sometimes.
On second thought, don't bring any children.

Come alone. Probably you don't even have children.
If your lab tests are correct there's a break
in your DNA. That's usually fatal though sometimes
it's a very good sign. The data is murky. Nobody knows
for sure if we're talking solution or problem.
If there's anything we don't understand here it's blood.

Many of our doctors faint at the sight of blood.
Really, 80% of them are worse than children.
We know this isn't your problem.
But it's a lot better when they take a golf break.
Then we write tons of letters like these. We know
how to run a front office. Sometimes

patients ask us for a diagnosis and sometimes
we guess right. No nasty stool samples or blood
tests. Often the patients themselves know
what's what. And every now and then clever children
will point out a suppurating wound or a break
in the ulna, which usually solves the problem.

Drop by on your next coffee break. Everybody has problems.
Yours is not taxes but blood. Bring about a quart. It's probably
nothing, but don't let the children know quite yet.

Jealousy

"The scratching of the pen,
   the whisper of the pencil."

The epigraph comes from the only arresting line
in an otherwise bad novel in which the detective wrote poetry
when he wasn't solving crimes.

Summoned, he would lay aside the tools of one trade and pick
up those of the other: revolver and binoculars, revolver and micro-
cassette recorder, revolver and brass knuckles. But always
the revolver.

Jealousy was often involved. A married man with a mistress,
an older woman and her son's trophy wife. A horse breeder
and his neighbor's prized stallion.

To investigate, the detective would leave his study. Behind him
lay the poem he was working on: a large X through a small stanza,
synonyms in the margin looking askance at one another, the pen
scratching to be let in again, the pencil whispering, "No."

7:00 A.M. FLIGHT

I am stopped by a stern TSA employee and told to send
Nine Horses through the X-ray, too, behind
my shoes and jacket.

So the poems disappear in a gray, plastic craft of their own.
I stand with my arms out like a scarecrow and a uniformed
agent scowls at my socks.

Moments later, the book emerges like a young
scholar dozing in a weathered punt watching the blue
Cambridge sky through sun-dazed, half-closed eyes

until, just beyond the vicar's cottage, he is met by a friend
who helps him to his feet and says how pleased he is
to see him again.

PART 3

For 1-10, choose a, b, or c. You must choose one. No erasures.

1. After a trip to that soothsayer in Burbank,

    a. the flag of betterment snaps in the wind.
    b. gang signs appear in the snow.
    c. feigned surprise is all the rage.

2. After the ranting that seems to be coming from the stars,

    a. surprise valentines arrive.
    b. stranded travel writers give up and drink the water.
    c. it's time to see Mr. Cat.

3. After the heavy foliage has been dealt with,

    a. the earth changes its mind about gravity.
    b. someone finally reports that corpse on the subway.
    c. 72 new vendors are provisionally licensed.

4. After the papal tour skirted Honduras,

    a. 1,000 pieceworkers leaned into their Singers.
    b. Bob's wife calls Connor's wife about the lucre.
    c. what's out in the dark becomes afraid of the dark.

5. After that rather surprising burst of laughter,

    a. parameters called it quits.
    b. there occurred a vast unfurling of wings.
    c. the bearded garden gnomes were taken in and fingerprinted.

6. After the heirloom napkins were soiled,

    a. it was time to mentally undress that sassy nephew.
    b. the debate over hi-jinks vs. terrorism continued.
    c. someone put down *The Portable Dos Passos* and sighed.

7. After the secrets of the world were exposed as claptrap,

    a. two or three cleansing breaths seemed to help.
    b. people gathered in the wrong waiting room but the right hospital.
    c. the allure of ordinary statues increased tenfold.

8. After the newlyweds slipped in the shower,

    a. the light around 4:00 p.m. was more intoxicating than usual.
    b. the Ouija spelled out "I marred you for luv."
    c. some folks could but didn't. Others did but shouldn't have.

9. After the true danger of beauty has been revealed,

    a. old-fashioned peep-shows open on nearly every corner.
    b. that barista at Starbucks relaxes with an orange Fanta.
    c. a direction called Never Coming Back appears on AAA maps.

10. After even the anchorman weeps at such a short list of survivors,

    a. Scrooge McDuck schedules a conference call.
    b. that anonymous creep identifies himself as "maybe Ted."
    c. the *Norton Anthology* on the futon opens itself to an ode.

The Ogre's Wife

I don't remember being little, growing up, having friends
over, much less opening the door for ogre suitors
clutching limp bouquets in their huge, hot hands.

I seem to have always been what I am: the ogre's wife.

This much I know: he hates it when I think. He wants
his dinner, he wants to count his gold, he wants to snore.
He'd beat me if he knew I was writing this in blood

on the cutting board, but I like to see my thoughts
laid out until the house starts to shake and a cup
of water washes them all away.

He throws open the door and drops something
on the table: a cow or a limp boy in the clothes
his mother made for him.

I've walked to the end of the straight road, and it
just stops. When I looked down, nothing but the tops
of clouds.

What am I to do except stoke the fire, feed it with
the homespun pants and shirt, wash the almost perfect
body, then sharpen my knife.

From the other room comes the clink of coins, plop
of another priceless egg, his command to "Play!"
then the harp eking out the only song it knows.

Tales of the Christian Martyrs

It's my turn to sit with Sebastian whose wife
left him. We're on the old couch in his new
apartment watching *Last Train From Gun Hill.*

Lately he likes anything that's noisy and mean
even though he's skinny and mild, and now
that I think of it looks a little like St. Sebastian,
the one with all the arrows

which reminds me that once in a pub Sheila
hurled a real dart at him and Sebastian walked
around for half an hour with it stuck in his shoulder
until Brenda made him take it out.

Speaking of Brenda, she was over last night
and brought a casserole. Sebastian wouldn't
eat very much, she said, so I should try again.

But really I don't care if he ever eats.
When I was with Brenda, she never cooked.

"That panting on the wall"
really was the most interesting line
in the whole magazine.

But my pleasure in it was diminished
by the abject apology in the next issue:
Apparently the poet is still lying down
due to the typo that turned *painting*
into *panting.*

My disappointment was offset though
by a new poet who went on and on
about the waning light across harrowed
fields and the long shadows of cedar
and pine until finally everything
was "covered by dorkness."

ORNITHOLOGY

Walking toward the library, I pass three children
staring at a dead crow and daring each other
to poke it with a stick.

I stop, too, because I know a little about crows—
how, for instance, they are different from ravens.
I could tell these well-dressed children a lot.

Ravens are black with a purple tint while crows
are denied that royal hue. A crow's tale is squared-off
like the crew-cut on the boy at Menchie's who hands
them the expensive frozen yogurt

while a raven's tale is triangular, a shape discovered
by the Persians and beloved by the 17th century
mathematician Blaise Pascal. Furthermore, ravens
love solitude and prefer remote hills and woods
while a crow will perch on a stop sign and brag
about it endlessly.

But that isn't what they are concerned about.
They want to know about Death. And for that
I would have to fetch the skull from my desktop
and ask the sun to hide its face behind a dark,
galleon-shaped cloud and then—

Oh, wait. They're offering me the stick. All
they really want to know is will I poke the corpse.

Of course. And when I do and it moves, they
run away shrieking and delighted. More alive,
if possible, than before.

THE GINGERBREAD MAN

This is not the one about the childless couple and the cookie
that leapt from the oven and ran away from everyone
and everything but the fox.

This is the one about the woman who, while her husband was
snoring, baked a burly gingerbread man. Piece by piece.
Arms and legs, pelvis and chest. And then assembled him
in a kitchen illuminated only by lightning.

He was wonderful: tall and dark with penetrating eyes
and a wry smile. She lay down on him. It was simultaneously
intoxicating and melancholy. She knew it couldn't last.

A night or two later while she was caressing her lover
she knocked over a wine glass and in came her husband
in his nightshirt to see what was happening.

Immediately he knew what to do: he started at the rival's
toes and began to eat. His wife watched, horrified and
excited. Legs and thighs, belly and arms, eyes and nose.
And then he kissed her with what had become the sweetest
lips in the world.

THE DOCENT

The table is from IKEA, but those napkin
rings were forged from jailers' keys. Owen
gave them to me as a gesture of friendship,
because that's what we are. Friends.
Well, once or twice we . . . You know
what? Let's just go into the kitchen.

Nothing ever happened here, on the floor
or in that windowed nook. My life isn't
an Italian movie. Not since Sergio left.

And here's the bedroom. Do you like
those Popeye sheets? I couldn't resist
and they were on sale. Ensign Salter calls
me his little Olive Oyl.

Let's just peek into the bathroom. I love
those koi on my shower curtain. Hiroki
says they look real. He's been a tower
of strength through some difficult times
and he does have the most beautiful hair.

Well, we're back where we started. It's
been a pleasure. Can I offer you something
to drink? It's dusk, not my favorite time.
Why don't you stay.

ALONE

Maybe it's just the kind of poetry I've been reading,
but I can't help noticing how alone most poets are:

alone in a room, of course, furnished with only
a picture of Virginia Woolf. Alone in Paris or Corfu,
alone by a famous grave in an equally famous mist.

Do I have to say alone in a crowd? And, to update
the image, all alone by the iPhone. Oh, let's not
forget the sea.

Those solitary walks on the beach. The moon-blanched
land and the way the body of Matthew Arnold always
washes up at the poet's bare feet.

I could compile an anthology of poems about being
alone. Now that I think of it, *Being Alone* might be
a wonderful title.

It would be fun to write to all the poets and get
permission to use their work. Even more fun
to have a big party and hammer out the details.

Let's see—I'd need a lot of alcohol and a ton
of things to eat. Clean sheets for the spare bedrooms
for sure because you know how poets are:

when they get together, they can't keep their hands
off each other.

THE TROJAN PONY

There it sits one morning shining in the sun.
A giant toy. Beyond inviting. Irresistible.

The Trojan children haul it around back.
They make their toy ponies rear and whinny

and eventually kneel. They do this until nap
time, then drink juice and stretch out in the sun.

Pretty soon the Greek children emerge.
"We win!" they shout standing over the Trojans

who look pleased and surprised. A blonde girl
timidly offers half a cookie and the victor

gobbles it up even as he continues to
brandish his enormous cardboard sword.

The Invisible Man

and his wife have a child. So cute. She sucks her invisible
thumb. Finds her invisible feet.

She's struck by an invisible pathogen. What to do? There is
no invisible doctor.

Helplessly they watch her expire. At the funeral, two
handkerchiefs ascend, descend, ascend.

The Invisible Man feels mean. Betrayed. He'll show them.
No more making a hat dance

down the street. No more snatching someone's milkshake.
Strychnine in a cocktail,

tinkering with the tour bus's brakes, a nudge on the surgeon's
elbow. Revenge will keep him busy.

But what about his wife home all day alone. That empty
crib below a mobile of plastic question

marks and ampersands that the baby liked to breathe on
and then, helplessly, reach for.

Taken according to directions, Maximinn is perfectly safe and effective. Well, not perfectly safe. Nothing's perfect. Almost safe. Nearly. Nine times out of ten. Or six times. It depends. Naturally there are side effects. The most common is not anal leakage. There are a lot worse things than that. Otherwise clinical trials would be open to the public. There may be gastrointestinal events, however. If you are carrying cash or a passport in one of those pouches that tuck inside your pants, we suggest you find a safer place. During cold weather, your toes may hurt and there could be problems passing urine. If either occurs, tell your doctor immediately! If you can see him, since vision changes and eye pain are common. Not common, exactly. More like—Well, okay. Common.

Maximinn must not be used by female patients who have children or may want to have children. Or who may enjoy sex on their hands and knees. There is just something about that position that renders Maximinn lethal. Male patients may enjoy themselves but prolonged use of Maximinn makes them prone to an oral discharge called Black Throat, so no kissing. Not that anybody would want to. Of course new troubles can crop up later. Much later. Barking and hair loss, for example. This is called off-target activity and is difficult to predict. Actually, impossible.

Ask your doctor if Maximinn is right for you.

THE GARDENER'S FUNERAL

There were some real barrio moguls: shaved heads,
prison tatts. But behaving themselves. "Housebroken
cobras," as Lorca liked to say.

The animals that are our bodies prowled for awhile,
then I stood under power lines beside a girl
with a bleeding heart and a lacy bra.

The trees were close but looked far away and painted
on the sky.

When it was my turn with the widow I pronounced the hard
consonants of my name. "Ah, *si*," she said. "You have
the bougainvillea *tan bella*."

Santiago's body was elsewhere in a suit, probably
with a handkerchief over his face.

I ate everything anyone handed me, then said good night
a hundred times.

Past the kids with a soccer ball, past the babies saying
their secret names, across Rooster Comb bridge,

all the way to my beautiful bougainvillea that will
soon need pruning.

The Death of Hansel

Gretel enrolls in night school. A creative writing class.
There are other women in their fifties. One keeps pointing
her expensive breasts at the teacher. One has crazy hair
and a pentagram. They're nice enough, though.

Gretel likes to sit with the young people. The girls treat
her like a mom, spilling all kinds of secrets. Their idea
of an endearment is to give her a joint or two
in a Sucrets box.

Gretel likes the class. The teacher is bigger than she
expected, strong like a woodsman. She's sorry when
he hands out the last poem.

At home, she sits in the window seat and smokes.
The marijuana makes her sleep and before that she
feels—she learned this word recently—phantasmagorical.

The moon is either there or she knows where it is.
A forest fills her little yard. A trail of white pebbles
leads God-knows-where. She lets herself cry once
a week and this is the time.

"Oh, honey," she says. "I miss you so much."

Museum of Science & Industry

Most of us who worked there came in slightly hung over.
It helped as we sorted through the shabby uniforms we had
to wear, an enterprise tantamount to turning the pages
of the only novel in the world.

And then it was upstairs, through the quiet halls, under
the photos of the famous, past the resting turbines and looms
to make sure no one touched the Van de Graff generator
or interrupted the life cycle of the salmon.

At eleven sharp, hundreds of school children poured off
of buses along with their teachers, their soft purses bulging
with Saltines and Kleenex.

Sometimes I thought about sleeping with these young women,
taking off the wraparound skirts and modest shoes, then later
listening to them talk about their students, last names first.

Often, though, I imagined merely dancing with them.
Not in a club but right there in the Museum of Science & Industry,
stunning the entire first grade as we waltzed around the room.
Above us Madame Curie scowled down but Descartes,
who had written "Passions of the Soul," smiled benevolently.

Icarus

Forget the version with the wax wings. Forget the painting
by Bruegel and the poem by Auden.

Icarus and his father escape from Crete by boat. Daedalus
invents sails to outrun King Minos' galleys.

Icarus prances around the stern giving Cretans the finger
and at some point falls overboard.

He's not missed immediately and when he is it's too late.
Daedalus grieves. The others lie

on the deck eating the biscuits and honey Icarus had
in his rucksack. Drinking his water.

How amazing to go so fast without rowing!

Burning the Book

The anthology of love poems I bought
for a quarter is brittle, anyway, and comes
apart when I read it.

One at a time, I throw pages on the fire
and watch smoke make its way up
and out.

I'm almost to the index when I hear
a murmuring in the street. My neighbors
are watching it snow.

I put on my blue jacket and join them.
The children stand with their mouths
open.

I can see nouns—*longing, rapture, bliss*—
land on every tongue, then disappear.

Bad News About My Vocation

I remember how the upper crust in my hometown
pronounced it—care-a-mel. Which is correct, I guess,
but to everybody else it was carmel.

Which led to the misconception about the order
of Carmelites.

I imagined they served God by heating sugar
to about 170 C, then adding milk and butter
and vanilla essence while they listened
to the radio.

I thought I could do that. I could wear the white
shirt and pants. I knew I couldn't be good
but I might be a good candy maker.

So imagine my chagrin when I learned about
the vows of poverty and toil enjoined
by these particular friars.

I also crossed off my list the Marshmellowites
and the Applepieites, two other orders I
was thinking of joining.

Little, Small, Wee Bear

The rangers may have to shoot the grizzly
who's terrorizing campers down by Tower
Falls. The snuffle in the night, the nose
beneath the flap, the way he maims their
victuals and then mounts the mini-van
looking for a toe-hold in that other world,
the one he strolled in while the porridge cooled.

Pretty soon, though, he is great and huge.
The cottage and the comfy chair are nothing
but a hum that makes him swat his head
until it's gone and he's stopped thinking
about her. Then the tattered cots remind him
he had a bed and she was in it, hair yellow
as mustard weed. And the rampage begins.

Jaguar Gentlemen's Club

The jaguars in this place are very mild
not like the animated neon sign
that advertises college girls gone wild.

The waitresses are slower than the Nile
and mostly they resemble javelin.
The jaguars in this place are very mild.

My lap dance girl was once a foster child.
She tells me this and takes an aspirin
like lots of tipsy college girls gone wild.

But she turns out to be so free of guile
we chat about my cousin Mary Finn.
The jaguars in this club are very mild.

Guess what! She knew my roommate as a child.
Both born and raised in chilly Michigan,
too cold a place for going really wild.

Mostly I just watch, a lazy crocodile.
I wallow in this ersatz pool of sin.
The jaguars in this club are very mild,
despite the ads for college girls gone wild.

A Page from the Apocrypha

So God throws Adam and Eve out of paradise
but they don't slink away wailing and ashamed
like the characters in Italian frescoes.

Instead, Adam turns and says, "Ah, You big lug.
I've been eighty-sixed from a lot better places than
this king-sized salad bar."

Eve starts to laugh, something she's never
done before since there's nothing funny
about perfection.

Adam winks at her and laughs, too.
His hand smoothes her hair. Hers touches
his chest. All of a sudden they're kissing
and looking for a place to lie down.

It's chilly, the ground is brambly and damp,
but they don't care. They're in love.

Not the God-kind, all infinite numbers and
tranquility. But the human-kind, perilous
and messy, the kind that makes you want
to live forever.

Three Haibun

I

10:00 a.m. Time for a Dr. Pepper, the friendly pepper-upper, compared
to the more quarrelsome brands. Outside the big window, Tony edits
my lawn, going margin-to-margin with his green mower. I take him a
cold drink as he stops to rake around the spring bulbs that have shot up,
and when he asks what that big one is I tell him Amaryllis fell in love
with a gardener. To impress him, she stabbed herself in the heart
a little every day. Each drop of blood made a new, beautiful flower.
Tony says, "That's a story, right?" Overhead, police and news copters
hover. At eye level a hummingbird looks me in the retina for a split second.
Macro and micro. While Tony blows leaves around like the west wind,
I inspect my lawn, newly drought-resistant like some people I know who
live alone or with somebody dreadful and not only survive but flourish.
When Tony's son was sick and in County USC, a Hispanic intern took
him aside and said, "Anywhere but here, amigo." Yet Anthony got well
and is back in school thanks to a delicate operation performed by a surgeon
with a long last name. "Not a cowboy Indian," Tony says. "The other kind."
His cell jangles, he returns the still-cool bottle, and speeds away. The honey-
suckle sticks out its tongue at me. A ladybug lights on my hand, checks
things out, then rests on my ring finger where it looks stunning.

I miss the old phones,
twining my fingers around
the cord as I begged.

II

2:00 p.m. Driving fast, I pass Ronald McDonald House where a woman
in a yellow two-piece swim suit suns herself on the Saint Augustine lawn.
Usually that's peopled with parents and their bald children. This lady is
merely working on her tan. "Now," said Tolstoy, "is the only time over
which we have dominion." Uptown, the clothes in Banana Republic
are lit by candlelight since a transformer has blown, and all of Colorado
Boulevard is without power. It is like shopping in beautiful ruins and
"all the air a solemn stillness holds," as Thomas Gray said in another
context. We pay in cash or write checks, the surly clerks soften and stop
yearning to be in France or on TV. Even the traffic hums on key as I
motor home. Pulling into my driveway, I have to brake for the homeless
woman who lives in the bushes by the library. Most citizens consider
her an eyesore. I wonder if she's like those ornamental hermits of the
eighteenth century who were paid to be melancholy. But by whom?

Taking out the trash,
there are those stained glass windows
too red to believe.

III

4:00 p.m. The last Dr. Pepper of the day, this time on the porch. Ten yards
away, three high school kids have what my mother would call "ants in their
pants." They are squirming and passing the new yearbook around. Now I
am carried back into the past and my classmates: Kay with her portable
radio covered in white leather like a good girl's Bible. She toted it to the
plunge but kept a towel over it thus the race music pouring out of it was
slightly de-fanged. Alfred who was the laughing-stock of C.H.S. compared
to Joseph Lawrence, the class clown. Randy Diaz who got handsomer by
the minute. Anita George who loved the Antlers in the Treetops jokes and
French-kissed everybody. And more, of course—the despised and sultry, the
ordinary and the immortal. Time to declare martial law on Memory and get
it home before nightfall. Those kids on the sidewalk are all on their phones
now. Conversations drift up like smoke from separate cook-outs: kosher,
vegan, and eat-what's-on-your-plate-or shut-up.

A thousand years slip
by. Stamps are obsolete. Still,
notes get passed around.

III

The Cowboy Poet Considers
His Uncollected Poems

I can see them from the porch sometimes
and they look mighty thin.

They're skittish, that's for sure. They'll come as far
as the fence but every step I take toward them
they take two back.

Sometimes the dog goes out on his own and rounds
up one I barely recognize.

I let him cool out, toss in some alfalfa. He's wary
and keeps to himself.

He needs his hooves trimmed and some Baytril
but you try and get in there with a rasp and
a syringe.

Pretty soon he looks goddamn miserable, so one
fine night I leave the gate open a tinch
and when I turn my back

he's gone.

Photo

There is the poet on the flyleaf
in the back. He's been waiting to greet
me when I finish the very last stanza then
pause to contemplate the great themes
of poetry: epiphany, love & sex, the beauty
of things, and—of course—death.

I was about to get up and let the dog
out but that will have to wait while I
inspect the poet. His gaze is forthright
and warm. I like his two shirts, dark
over light. And look how one sleeve
rides up to reveal a watch registering
3:15 forever.

Now the dog is scratching at
the scarred door, so out he goes! Just as
I imagine the poet at 3:30 or 4:00 released
from the studio with its black backgrounds,
the snap and tic of its huge, cooling lights.

Maybe the poet has a drink, covers
two lines in his notebook, or meets
someone in a bar with stenciled cranes
on the wall, cranes that throw back their
heads and cry *Now Now.*

Here I whistle for the dog,
but he refuses. It's all too wonderful—
trees and cars, little cadavers the cats
leave, a soiled bag of god-knows-what
that he can't wait to sink his teeth into.

JACK

After that dead giant gets hauled away, it's just
Mother and me. And the gold.

I buy some new clothes, drop in at the pub.
Girls sit on my lap and tell me I'm handsome.
Then I pick up the tab. If I don't, they pout.

Strangers stop me with the saddest stories I've
ever heard. But I can't give everybody a golden
egg. She might be a magic hen, but she's still a hen.

So I get the cold shoulder. And graffiti on the new
fence. UP YOUR BEANSTALK! And it isn't just
a fence. It's a wall. Which we need because
of the robberies.

Last week somebody snatched the harp. "Master!
Master!" it cried. I leaped out of bed, got off a shot
or two and whoever it was fled empty-handed.

I used to be a thief in that world above the clouds.
The giant's wife hid me and coddled me. Now look.
I'm a fat man in silk pajamas holding a gun.

"Favorites Win Only 33% of the Time"

Handicapper's Digest

Let's do the math—if there are nine races a day, there are nine
favorites, so six of them will lose. Easy money. Except it doesn't
work that way. The figures only hold up over time.
In the long run. Eventually.

Some days every favorite wins, prancing home to pay $3.40
bathed in that special borealis light the chosen can emit.
While other days every favorite returns to the back stretch
and mopes in the corner of his stall.

Horses aren't stupid. They know when they have let everyone
down. They know they eat a lot and need many shoes. All they
have to do is run, and some days it just isn't fast enough.

That is why some horses learn to play the accordion, to endear
themselves to the humans who care for them. A soulful rendition
of *Los Bracheros* reminds Enrique, Hector and Guillermo of home,
so they are free to weep openly

and even in an office festooned with halters, bridles, and whips
the trainer hears the melancholy strains and thinks, "He's a pretty
good old horse sometimes."

DEAR CONSUMER

The assembly instructions you received with your most
recent purchase were meant for a different item. The swing
set you ordered does not need a radioactive titanium rod.
Please return that in the lead-lined protective container enclosed.
Two pairs of disposable gloves are also included. Wear both
pairs. They have textured surfaces for maximum grip and 0.007"
fingertip thickness for maximum tactile sensitivity. Do not
return the gloves with the radioactive core. Keep them with
our compliments. You may or may not have also received
a DVD entitled "Building Your Own Nuclear Device."
We hope not. Just destroy that. Do not return it. It is not ours.
It never was.

One in ten consumers who ordered The Swingeroo Swing Set
were contacted by the president of an organization called Hot
Lifestyles. We do not know how this happened. Our sincere
apologies. Please—simply enjoy your backyard swing set
with one caveat. A few, a very few, tend to collapse due to
metal stress issues in the suspension system. Nobody's perfect.
If you will return the set in its original packing with appropriate
paperwork (BOL, SCAC, pro number, etc.) we will see what,
if anything, can be done.

ADVICE TO A YOUNG POET

Fuck all the gloomy insight.
Fuck the high seriousness.
And fuck those whispers in the night.

No goddamned ebbing of the light,
either. Tell me about your mattress
and how it's not quite right.

Did you trash your kid's new kite?
Good. That's all you get to confess
to. Nobody cares if you're contrite

or if you regularly weep at midnight.
And for Christ's sake no "opalesce"
and fuck the fucking candlelight,

too. Start a line with tons of dynamite
instead. Talk about an actress
with nice tits. Stop being polite!

An M.A. by mail makes you erudite.
Show some guts and stab a shepherdess.
Fuck all the gloomy insight.
And fuck those whispers in the night.

OPEN AT 10:00 A.M.

I burst in at 10:01 and surprise
the pretty clerks whispering,
giggling, fussing with each other's
hair, holding out their pale wrists
suffused with the newest scent.

Everybody blushes as I stare.
I feel like one of the characters
of mythology stumbling upon
naiads bathing. But not Acteon
with his ravenous hounds.

Just a bumpkin standing by
the water's edge, one hand
on the warm flank of his
lost cow.

The Suitors

After Ulysses had been gone a long time, the suitors came.
At first just a few. They actually liked Penelope and could
stand her son Telemachus.

She was a peach, and grief just made her somehow peachier.
The suitors were young, too. They walked around half-naked
and wrestled each other

covered with oil. The winners looked up at her windows
and crowed. Years passed, poems and compliments dried up.
The suitors got fat drinking

her wine. They started sleeping with the servant girls. Then
Homer says Penelope longed to "display herself to her suitors,
fan their hearts, inflame

them more." Who could blame her? She wasn't getting any
younger. Some of the suitors were cute and lied well.
She had needs. But there

was Argus, Ulysses' faithful dog. Always staring at the sea.
Waiting. It was Argus who kept her on the straight and narrow.
If he could do it,

so could she. He slept beside her bed and when she got up
to pee followed her and licked her feet and when she wept
put his head on her bare knees.

And then Ulysses returned. Dressed as a beggar, but she knew,
so she said she would marry the one who could string
Ulysses' bow. Only

he could do that. When the suitors saw it, they started to pack,
but it was too late. Ulysses killed them all. Every one
who had teased her and eaten her

out of house and home and corrupted her servants. She watched
him do it. There was blood everywhere. And it made her
heart beat fast.

She enjoyed the carnage, but longed to take her husband
into the bedroom. On his side of the bed, the pillow was,
even after twenty years, still plump and cool.

THE GHOST IS COUGHING

pretty badly, so my wife calls his mother then
puts him on the couch under my favorite quilt
as the trick-or-treaters outside demand candy.

I'm just glad the real monsters aren't at my door:
Frankenstein with stomach flu? She'd say,
"Come on in." Ditto for a feverish Wolfman
or any zombie with a rapid heartbeat.

Into the kitchen they go: chicken soup by
the quart, plenty of vitamin C, naps
in front of the fire.

Pretty soon they feel better and the Mummy
in his new bandages wants to carry her back
to the tomb while the Creature from the Black
Lagoon keeps turning up in the shower.

I plead with her, "You've got to get rid
of these monsters."

She waits till midnight. One last Bloody Mary
for Dracula and I point to the door.

"You guys are going to be fine," she says.
"You're super-scary again. I'm terrified.
Really."

She stands on the porch until they get to
the corner and she's sure they've crossed
safely and disappeared into the dark
where they belong.

THERE'S THIS GUY WITH ONE ARM

who owns the corner of Pasadena Ave. and Del Mar.
He doesn't have a cardboard sign, just a bucket of water
and a squeegee.

He's fast and efficient, working against time condensed
to red light/green light.

The guy in the Volvo keeps pointing to streaks. Then instead
of handing over a dollar, he tosses and it blows away.

The one-armed man yells, the driver rolls his
window all the way down and yells back. I get out
of the car to lend, well, a hand I guess.

Just then the light changes its mind. There are twenty
cars behind me, nineteen of them complaining.

It's always like that, isn't it. Red light/green light.
Red light/green light.

Solitude

The storm is over and I am powerless. Around me,
though, other houses glow. Their bedrooms, still
in disarray, are warm to the touch.

I have to admit it is pleasant to stand in the dim
kitchen and heat yesterday's coffee in a saucepan.
No one can call me with a voice full of tears.
No accusations from red lips, a tiny phone lost
in a cloud of dark hair.

How simple to wash a dish or two and dry them
with a new white towel. Then feed the cat, years ago
freed from the distractions of the carnal.

Look how he watches as I mimic the eunuchs
of the T'ang Dynasty who wrote poems on red leaves
and floated them to the external world in the water
of the palace garden channel.

Cavafy Latte

Everybody's talking about Shaunelle. It's been a week now,
five days for sure, and she hasn't come in to hold court
at the table by the door. Her table.

She'd appear about noon disheveled, usually with some bare flesh
showing even on chilly days. She often looked feverish but beautiful
despite the tattoos—the koi and the sacred heart. Or because of them.

She liked good-looking boys and if she went with anybody else
it was for reasons of her own. The scorned said it was for a meal
or a joyride. But they were jealous and confused. After all, she'd
taken their cigarettes and in one case a turquoise scarf.

Her behavior wasn't wise or prudent. There were people, girls
especially, who wouldn't sit with her. But boys talk and it's not
always blasphemy. Arnie's hands tremble when he remembers,
and twice already today Vince has told about letting Shaunelle
win at cards and, though all she did was kiss him and that a result
of high spirits only, it was so genuine and passionate he can't
put it out of his mind.

Certainly I wish I had known her better, but being neither good-
looking nor fortunate, I am exempt from her tyranny though
I am as naked under my clothes as she.

BEAUTY AND THE BEAST

Oh, god. He's horrible. And he smells!
He sits on his haunches. But he talks.
"Are you well?" *Yes.* "Is everything to
your liking?" *Yes.* "Will you marry me?"
No. "In that case, Beauty, good night."

Every evening he watches her eat and they
chat. Should the red flowers be more red
or less? What if the snow was warm?
Are there enough swans? "Will you marry
me, Beauty?" "No, Beast." "In that case,
good night."

Eventually she asks to see her family.
Her sisters are busy flirting and preening.
Her father is dating a girl half his age. And
the night is just night, not like there where
it's silk with a crimson tint.

She twists the ring he gave her. She says,
"I wish to return to my palace and see my
Beast again." And bingo! She's back
quicker than e-mail.

He's almost dead, but the sound of her
voice revives him and he gasps, "Will
you marry me?"

A willing "Yes," and then the kiss that
changes everything. He isn't a beast
anymore—passionate and dangerous.
Just a boy with hands and feet and perfect
little teeth, a boy who can't stop looking
at himself in the mirror.

Judas Goat

The summer I worked for Armour Meats I'd be on my way
to the billing department. In the holding pens, sheep were
settling down behind a mild-mannered goat who with his

little beard looked like a classics professor in a small
private college about to lead sophomore girls into
the *Inferno*.

That would be 1962. Uncle Jack was still alive. He flew
B42s in WWII, mission after mission, until his nerves
were shot. He couldn't sleep and shook so bad his bed
moved.

But the Air Force, like Armour Meats, found a job for him.
He could fly the assembly ship, usually a battered old
Liberator decorated with checks and polka-dots and stripes

like a crazy fat person. A plane like that could be seen
for miles and bombers from various air bases would fall
in behind him.

He'd lead the formation almost to the target, then slowly
turn toward home. "Jesus Christ, it was awful. I had
a navigator and a co-pilot and we couldn't look at each
other."

His hands still shook as he reached for the lamb chops
I brought home, the ones my mother had to cut up for him.

I Like to Iron

The shades are drawn. The cat doesn't care.
I've got a spray bottle and a hot Sunbeam.
I'm going to town when there's a knock

at the door and it's Death. "I'm all wrinkled,"
Death says. He shows me some hem and
sleeve. "Hand it over," I say. "Turn

your back," he says. Pretty soon the cloak
oozes across my shoulder. The cloth is rich
and good and holds a crease.

I fling it back and hear him shimmy.
"Obliged," he says. And takes his leave.
I listen for the skid or shot.

The neighborhood is asleep except
for one antsy kid in her hopscotch
house, safe as safe can be.

I was with older boys. Going on dangerous rides, eating terrible things on a stick. Staring at the girls they stared at. "Look as old as you can," one of them told me, and we filed into French Follies. I liked standing in sawdust because it made me feel like a 4H animal. The show was just one girl after another taking off her costume until she was naked. Then she stood there chewing her gum, both hands on her hips in an I-dare-you-pose. The last one wasn't dressed like a harem girl but like a real person. She stepped out of her dress and sighed. Took off her brassiere and sniffed it. "I can see this crap at home," somebody muttered. A tattooed man in a dirty shirt walked out onto the stage. He had a piece of lead pipe in one hand and he slapped it into the palm of the other. "She's tired tonight," he explained. The whiner said, "I can get that at home, too." "Why don't you come on up here and formally lodge a complaint," said the on-stage man. Outside, someone strong rang the bell, someone screamed as the red car plummeted.

WALT WHITMAN IN NORTH HOLLYWOOD

The half-open door invites him, so he steps in, hands calloused
and strong, hat adjusted rakishly.

He rates a glance from one or two on the set, a PA or 2nd AD
but WW does not have the ferociousness of the Mid-West
father come to find his errant child.

He may just be someone setting something down
        or picking something up.

His smile is open and curious as he surveys the naked bodies
and the bed like a highway with many commuters full in size,
immodest and licentious
        mouthing their happiness.

He thinks back to his correspondence with Sergeant Thomas
P. Sawyer of the Eleventh Massachusetts Infantry, the letters
        strange and unusual and mostly misunderstood.

This love so public and casual charms him. The suitors and
swains, the tomboy and vamp—hair both flaxen
        and buckwheat

yet even as the smoke from cigarettes rises as if from
the trimmed lamps of oracles their hearts cry out.

Only he hears beneath the prickly sarcasm and rude jest
the way the slant rhymes of memory fall into place—

drawstrings of their night clothes undone by strange, large
hands and the smoky breath with scythe-like
        whispers as he (it is usually but not always a he)

asks and waits not but mauls and plows and dribbles
gibberish.

Don't they then sprawled like this resemble soldiers
in the hospitals at Arlington with jaundiced eyes
         and feverish lips to whom he brought savory
         morsels, oranges and figs.

His heart opens. He would clasp hands with them if he
could even as from a distance he enjoys the endless noon
         of the key light and smiles at the prostitute—
because is that not what she is and is that not holy too?—
who accepts a dark blue robe from a maiden busy yet
         bashful clutching a clipboard and watch.

In them all runs the same blood as politicians and preachers.
The soul is always full of sweetness. The brackish waters
         of the past cannot wash that away.

During a disagreement, WW sighs. In vain, in vain. How
everything struggles—man vs. man vs. woman, the cow
         and the border collie, the gardener and the grass.

Who is not sulky, dissatisfied, intolerant as well as ample,
hot-blooded and prosperous?

Now they eye him curiously. It is his look, vigorous and calm.
His very mien. Understanding rises out of him like a fragrant
mist.

Someone calls for quiet. The pulling and hauling begins.
Flesh swells. Cries like those of the gull or partridge.

BIOGRAPHICAL NOTE

Ron Koertge teaches at Hamline University in their low-residency MFA program for Children's Writing. A prolific writer, he has been published widely in such seminal magazines as *Kayak* and *Poetry Now*. Sumac Press issued *The Father Poems* in 1973, which was followed by many more books of poetry including *Fever* (Red Hen Press 2007), *Indigo* (Red Hen Press 2009), and *Lies, Knives and Girls in Red Dresses* (Candlewick Press 2012). He is a contributor to many anthologies, such as Billy Collins' *Poetry 180* and Kirby & Hamby's *Seriously Funny*. Koertge also writes fiction for teenagers, including many novels-in-verse: *The Brimstone Journals, Stoner & Spaz, Strays, Shakespeare Bats Cleanup,* and *Shakespeare Makes the Playoffs*. All were honored by the American Library Association and two received PEN awards. He is the recipient of grants from the NEA and the California Arts Council and has poems in two volumes of *Best American Poetry*.

Just as all water is holy water, so this pseudo-love with
its counterfeit-throes and imitative-desire is love.

"Hey, old man. Who let you in? The Senior Center is just
down the street, okay? No peeking!"

WW doffs his hat and smiles. His salute is returned two
dozen times as he retreats into this valley with a name—
San Fernando

all of it suffused now with crimson and scarlet as the workday
wanes and becomes dusk.